THE
★ *CALIFORNIA* ★
GOLD RUSH

by
LINDA THOMPSON

Rourke
Publishing LLC
Vero Beach, Florida 32964

www.rourkepublishing.com

PHOTO CREDITS:

Ayers, James J. Gold and Sunshine, *Reminiscences of Early California*, Illustrations from the Charles B. Turrill collection, 1922: pages 28, 30; Bonsal, Stephen, *Edward Fitzgerald Beale*, 1912: pages 6, 14, 20; Courtesy California Department of Conservation, California Geological Survey: pages 9, 12, 20, 32, 33; Courtesy Northwestern University Library, Edward S. Curtis Collection: page 6; Courtesy Library of Congress, Prints and Photographs Division: Cover, pages 5, 8, 11, 13, 19, 20, 22, 24, 27, 34, 43; Marryat Frank, *Mountains and Molehills*, 1855: Title Page, 10, 17, 19, 29, 37; Courtesy National Parks Service: page 27; Peters, DeWitt Clinton, *Kit Carson's Life and Adventures*, 1873: pages 16, 23; Russ, Carolyn Hale, *The Log of a Forty-Niner*, 1923: page 7; Courtesy Scotts Bluff National Monument: pages 4, 31, 35; Courtesy National Museum of Natural History, The Smithsonian Institution, James E. Taylor Collection: page 39; Courtesy HighMesaProductions.com: pages 25, 26-27, 40-41, 42.

SPECIAL NOTE: Further information about people's names shown in the text in bold can be found on page 44. More information about glossary terms in bold in the text can be found on pages 46 and 47.

DESIGN: ROHM PADILLA
LAYOUT/PRODUCTION: ELIZABETH BENDER

Library of Congress Cataloging-in-Publication Data

Thompson, Linda, 1941-
   The California Gold Rush / Linda Thompson.
         p. cm. -- (The expansion of America)
   Includes bibliographical references and index.
   ISBN 1-59515-222-9 (hardcover)
   1. California--Gold discoveries--Juvenile literature. I. Title. II.
Series: Thompson, Linda, 1941-   Expansion of America.
   F865.T47 2004
   979.4'04--dc22

                    2004009938

TITLE PAGE IMAGE
Illustration of a mining camp in the California mountains

TABLE OF CONTENTS

Only 20 years after it became independent, the United States gained a region that doubled the country's size. Barely 50 years later, it reached across immense plains and towering mountain ranges to touch the Pacific Ocean. How it grew so fast in such a short time is still an amazing tale.

(Left) James W. Marshall. (Below) painting of Marshall showing his find of gold to other workers

A single event on January 24, 1848—the discovery of gold in the **Sierra Nevada** foothills—brought thousands of people to the country's western shores. A New Jersey carpenter, **James W. Marshall**, was building a sawmill for a Swiss **immigrant** who was raising cattle on his ranch in northern California. At the time, California was a **province** of Mexico. But when Marshall looked into the river and saw something glitter, the timing of his discovery would prove to be very important.

Marshall spied the gold only nine days before California became United States territory. The **Mexican War** had recently ended. The United States gained the entire southwest, from New Mexico to the Pacific Ocean. The lure of gold—plus the appeal of living on American instead of Mexican soil—caused California's population to jump from 14,000 to 250,000 in only four years.

James W. Marshall in front of the sawmill where he originally found gold in 1848.

Native Americans, such as this man from the Tule River Reservation, saw their numbers decline sharply after the Gold Rush.

The population's basic **composition** also changed overnight. When California belonged to Mexico, **Hispanic** people made up at least 80 percent of the 14,000 non-Natives who lived there. Native Americans still numbered about 150,000, although their numbers were falling. The discovery of gold had disastrous effects on both Hispanic and Native populations. By 1870, Hispanics made up only 4% of the total population. Only 31,000 Native Californians remained among the total population of 380,000.

San Francisco in 1846 before the Gold Rush

Since there was no direct sailing route to San Francisco from the East, many ships had to brave the long journey around the tip of South America.

The Gold Rush brought an urgent need for better and faster ways to get messages, mail, and supplies to the thousands of people now living in the Far West. In 1849, it took up to four months for freight to reach San Francisco from the East. People and supplies had to travel nearly 2,000 miles (3,200 km) by trail from the Missouri River or 15,000 miles (24,100 km) by ship. Ships had to go around **Cape Horn** at the tip of South America, and many ships sank in storms before reaching their destination. The demand for **transcontinental** telegraph and rail connections became stronger every year.

"THE YELLOW METAL"

Gold is "the yellow metal that makes Wasichus [white men] crazy." —Black Elk, Sioux holy man.

By 1869, a new railroad linked the 3,500 miles (5,633 km) or more of wilderness between the east and west coasts of the United States. And when the century ended, 25 percent of the United States population lived west of the Mississippi. Within a few **decades**, improvements such as the railroad and the telegraph had made it much easier for those who settled the West to live comfortably in their adopted homelands.

Much of California had already been settled by the time the railroad linked the state to the rest of the country.

Chapter II: "I HAVE FOUND IT"

When Mexico became independent from Spain in 1821, fewer than 4,000 people lived in California, not counting the Native American population. At least two-thirds of these were women and children. Although more Mexicans moved north to "Alta California," the region did not attract many Americans because to own land they had to ask permission from Mexico City. But in 1839, one European, **John Sutter**, arrived. His name would forever be associated with the California Gold Rush.

Sutter had fled Switzerland to avoid **bankruptcy**, abandoning his wife and four children. He first worked as an innkeeper in Missouri so that he could acquire enough money to travel to Hawaii by ship and buy goods from the Far East. In Hawaii he convinced people that he was an important person seeking money for investments. Sutter became a Mexican citizen and settled on a 50,000-acre (20,250-hectare) ranch in northern California, which he named "**New Helvetia**." The site later grew into the city of Sacramento.

Before the Gold Rush started, the majority of miners in California were Spanish-speaking Californios.

9

THE CALIFORNIOS

The **Californios**, Spanish-speaking natives of California, needed very little money. From 1824 to 1847, Native Americans did almost all of the work. They tended crops, tanned hides, and worked as domestic servants. The **patron** of each **rancho** sold hides to passing ships and traded small amounts of gold and silver for luxury items. Many ranchos had mines because for centuries Mexicans had mined gold and silver. They sold small amounts or made it into jewelry, but kept the finds a secret out of fear that immigrants would overrun the country.

Native American and Californio with mule

The sawmill where Marshall found gold was east of Sutter's fort (above).

Sutter built an **adobe** fort and raised wheat and livestock. He planned to build a sawmill about 40 miles (64 km) to the east, near the present town of Coloma. This is where James W. Marshall, Sutter's builder, would find the **nugget** that set off the California Gold Rush.

While trying to get Sutter's sawmill finished before heavy rains came, James Marshall was concerned about the **tailrace**. A sawmill on a river uses the river's water to float logs and lumber and to drive the saw. A dam controls the flow of water. At Sutter's mill, the **headrace**—the water coming from the river above the mill—was working well, but the tailrace below the mill was too shallow and narrow. It had to be enlarged to produce enough water pressure to drive the saw.

THE WIMMER NUGGET

Peter Wimmer was head of the sawmill's construction crew and his wife, Elizabeth, was the cook. James Marshall asked Elizabeth to boil his nugget with some lye soap. This was a folk recipe for testing gold. The "Wimmer Nugget" weighed 7 grains (0.014 troy ounce or 0.454 gram). It is now in the University of California's Bancroft Library.

Example of a gold nugget

On January 24, 1848, Marshall was inspecting the lower end of the tailrace about 200 yards (20.1 m) from the mill. Something glittering in the gravel caught his eye. He picked up a piece and pounded it between two rocks. Like gold, it could be flattened but would not break. Marshall believed that the nugget was gold. "I have found it," he said when he arrived back at the mill. "I have found gold."

Marshall rode to New Helvetia to show Sutter the nugget. Following instructions found in an **encyclopedia**, they conducted tests. They put a sample in nitric acid, which did not affect it. They weighed the nugget and placed it on a set of scales, balanced by three silver dollars. They **submerged** the whole thing in water, and the scale containing the nugget sank, indicating a higher **density** for the gold.

QUALITIES OF GOLD

Gold is not affected by oxygen or common acids, so it is highly resistant to destruction. Most gold nuggets are 70 percent to 90 percent pure, usually mixed with silver. Gold is so moldable that one ounce of it can be hammered into a thin sheet that will cover 100 square feet (9.3 sq m). It is so **ductile** that one ounce can be stretched into a wire 50 miles (80.5 km) long. Gold is 19 times heavier than water, so it is said to have a **specific gravity** of 19. Its weight makes it quickly sink to the bottom when mixed with sand and gravel in a stream. Therefore, it can be separated easily from other materials, using a gold pan or a **sluice**.

Prospectors using the panning method to search for gold

13

Convinced it was real gold, Sutter hurried to prove his claim to the land. He drew up a **lease** and had the head of the local Native group, the **Coloma**, sign it. He then sent the document to Mexico's military commander at Monterey, along with a bottle of gold dust. But when his messenger reached Monterey, the Mexican commander rejected Sutter's claim to the ranch, arguing that Indians could not grant leases.

By this time word of the discovery was spreading. The messenger had bragged about the gold and showed it off. Even Sutter couldn't keep the secret, writing to his friend, General **Mariano Vallejo**, about the discovery. Still, it took months for anyone to pay attention. Because the **pioneers** who settled the West, especially newspaper writers and editors, liked to tell **tall tales**, people tended to doubt rumors of fantastic events such as this one.

Some men tried to profit from the Gold Rush in other ways, like building hotels and stores near the gold fields.

On March 15, 1848, nearly two months after Marshall's gold find, a notice about it appeared in *The Californian*, a San Francisco newspaper.

"GOLD MINE FOUND. In the newly made raceway of the Saw Mill recently erected by Captain Sutter, on the American Fork, gold has been found in considerable quantities. One person brought thirty dollars worth to New Helvetia, gathered there in a short time. California, no doubt, is rich in mineral wealth; great chances here for scientific capitalists."

Nobody reacted. Finally, a Mormon leader, **Samuel Brannan**, decided to visit New Helvetia and have a look at the gold. His plan was not to mine it himself but to profit from the miners who would soon flock to the area. Brannan began to construct a hotel and two stores near the gold fields, where he planned to trade merchandise for gold. On May 12, Brannan stood in San Francisco waving a bottle of gold dust and shouting "Gold from the American River!" By May 29, every man had left town! Soldiers and sailors deserted their posts, not even collecting their pay. News spread to Monterey, and that town was soon abandoned as well. Gold fever had hit California.

Kit Carson was the first to take word of the Gold Rush from Los Angeles across the country to Washington, D.C.

When the news reached Los Angeles, a well-known **mountain man** who had joined the Army happened to be in town. **Kit Carson** was the perfect messenger to rush the news to Washington, D.C. Nobody knew the trails as well as he did or could ride as fast. Carson set off for New Mexico, taking the Santa Fe Trail to Missouri. From there, he boarded a steamboat, arriving in Washington on August 2, nearly three months after he had left. He carried letters and a news article about the gold discovery.

Eastern editors were doubtful, and on August 19, the *New York Herald* published a story about the gold in the back pages. Very few readers took the news seriously or set off for California because of it.

Meanwhile, Colonel **Richard Mason**, a military commander and California's acting governor, had sent two messengers to Washington. The first left on August 30 by boat. Instead of going around South America, he got out at Panama and crossed the Isthmus of Panama, arriving in Washington on November 23. He carried some gold flakes and the Wimmer Nugget. The second messenger traveled overland, leaving on September 13 or 14, crossing Mexico, and arriving in Washington on November 22.

Travelers would cut out the trip around South America by crossing overland through Mexico or Panama. (Below) travelers crossing the Isthmus of Panama

President James K. Polk

POLK'S ADDRESS

"The accounts of the abundance of gold in that territory are of such an extraordinary character as would scarcely command belief were they not corroborated by the authentic reports of officers in the public service." —President Polk on December 5, 1848

A speedier messenger, sent by the Navy, raced across Mexico with news of gold and arrived first. On September 18, he met with President **James K. Polk**, who seemed not to believe him. But as more messengers arrived, all bearing the same news and samples of gold, President Polk finally believed the reports. On December 5, 1848, he announced the discovery to Congress and the nation. Now, eastern newspapers not only carried the story—they **exaggerated** it. New York's *Literary American* announced: "The streams [of California] are paved with gold—the mountains swell… it sparkles in the sands of the valley—it glitters in the **coronets** of the cliffs."

California **prospectors**, however, were already taking thousands of dollars worth of gold out of the American River.

Prospectors had already removed much gold before word even reached the East.

Within a few months, hundreds of people had begun to arrive from Hawaii, Oregon, Mexico, Chile, Peru, and Panama. But it was only after President Polk's speech that the real crowds headed west. Though slow to start, once it caught hold of people's imagination, gold fever could not be stopped.

Some newspapers ran stories telling how the land of California was made of gold.

WHAT SOME MINERS TOOK OUT

Early miners removed $4 million worth of gold by July 1848. One claim on the Yuba River that was 4 feet (1.22 m) square produced 30 pounds (13.6 kg). Gold went for about $16 an ounce (per 31.1 grams) at the time, and one 60-square-foot (5.6 sq m) claim produced $80,000 in six months. That would be about 112 pounds (50.8 kg), because gold is measured in **troy ounces**. "Troy" comes from Troyes, France, the site of a trade fair in the Middle Ages. A troy ounce is slightly heavier than an **avoirdupois** ounce and contains 12 ounces rather than 16. A troy ounce weighs 480 **grains** (31.1 grams).

Men working a plot of land with shovels and a sluice box

The discovery of gold at Sutter's sawmill changed traffic on the **Oregon Trail** forever. Previously, westbound settlers had mainly headed northwest toward Oregon's Willamette Valley. Now, thousands of wagons poured over the Sierra Nevada mountains, heading for the Sacramento Valley. The 400 California-bound people in 1848 became 30,000 in 1849 and 44,000 in 1850. These new pioneers were called "**forty-niners.**" They were also known as **argonauts**, after the crew of Jason's ship, *Argo*. In Greek **mythology**, Jason was a hero who, with the help of the gods found the golden fleece of a magical ram.

The crowded Oregon and California trails soon became littered with dead animals, bones, wagon parts, and discarded belongings. In 1850, 2,000 wagons were left in the California desert. Along the Nevada section of the trail, one traveler found 2,381 dead horses and mules, 433 dead or dying oxen, and 787 abandoned wagons.

A mining camp in California

21

Within one month of President Polk's announcement, 61 crowded ships were underway. More than 70 whaling ships were turned into passenger ships. Some of these, which had not been well maintained, sank in stormy seas on the way to San Francisco. The clipper ships were the fastest, arriving in only three months. The slowest trip, by paddle-wheel steamer, took nearly a year. The average journey was 115 days from Boston or New York.

(Above) Paddle-wheel steamboats were the slowest ships to arrive, and many ships were lost on the unpredictable sea.
(Below) the *Golden Gate* in the stormy waters of San Francisco Bay

The overland travelers left from Independence, St. Joseph, or St. Louis, Missouri. They bought covered wagons, oxen, horses, supplies, and food. Men rode beside the wagon train herding cattle. There was limited space in the wagons, so hundreds of people walked. Those who turned south took the Santa Fe Trail (and then the **Old Spanish Trail** from Santa Fe to California). A few argonauts went to Texas by boat, then rode or walked the **Sonora Trail** through Mexico to San Diego.

It was common for travelers to walk beside their wagons

Colt
revolver

People sold whatever they could, took their life savings, and set out by land or sea. Relatives, neighbors, or banks lent money for the trip, hoping to make a profit when gold was found. An early guidebook suggested taking $750 per person, though the average cost of the trip turned out to be $1,000.

The argonauts were well armed, carrying at least a revolver. Some added knives, walking sticks with concealed swords, or blackjacks in their hip pockets. Others carried a rifle or shotgun. They intended to protect their claims, shoot game, and kill Indians. Also, they had to defend themselves against a new kind of traveler—the trail robbers. These criminals planned to take miners' fortunes away by gambling, cheating, stealing, or any means they could.

Selling, trading, and gambling for gold at the El Dorado Hotel, Sacramento

OH SUSANNA

Miners sang the popular song *Oh! Susanna*, written by
Stephen Foster in 1848. But they made up lyrics more
suitable to gold mining, such as:
I soon shall be in Frisco
And there I'll look around
And when I see the gold lumps
there I'll pick them off the ground.
Oh! Susanna
Don't you cry for me
I'm off to California
With my washbowl on my knee.

Typical terrain of Death Valley, California

Native attacks on travelers were few, but thousands died of disease, mainly **cholera**. In 1849, a cholera **epidemic** moved up the Mississippi River from New Orleans and out along the Oregon Trail. One traveler wrote that in the first 170 miles (274 km), he saw four fresh graves every day. People also died from accidental shootings, hunger, thirst, or exposure to severe heat or cold. The challenges of the **terrain** were harsh. One area that Native Americans had named **Tomesha**, or "ground afire," was renamed Death Valley by argonauts in 1849. This valley in eastern California gets as hot as 134°F (56.7°C) in summer. Some groups of forty-niners survived only by climbing the steep mountains, where they could find cooler temperatures and water.

Once the gold-seekers reached San Francisco, living conditions were **dismal**. A huge city of tents appeared in the San Francisco hills. Overcrowding had pushed prices to new heights. A hotel room cost as much as $250 a week. In a rooming house, you could sleep against the wall for $8, with people packed in beside you and no bedding. If a miner was lucky enough to find a place to rent, he paid as much as $3,000 a month. If he wanted to buy land, he could get a 150-foot-(46-m-)wide lot for $8,000, which would have cost $20 a year before.

SAN FRANCISCO

In 1835, San Francisco (then called **Yerba Buena**) consisted of one family living in a tent beside the Bay. But by 1848, a year after being renamed San Francisco, it had become a small town. By the end of 1849, it had a population of 25,000—mostly men. Besides America, they came from Europe, Hawaii, Australia, New Zealand, the Middle East, South America, China, and other regions.

(Below) the entrance to San Francisco Bay before the Golden Gate Bridge was built

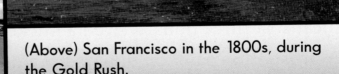

(Above) San Francisco in the 1800s, during the Gold Rush.
(Below) San Francisco in the 21st century

Ships in the harbor of New Helvetia during the Gold Rush

By 1850, more than 500 abandoned ships sat rotting in San Francisco Bay. Even the captains and crews had run off to the gold fields. Some ships were pushed ashore and made into buildings. One became a bank, another a church, and a third served as a prison.

Although a San Francisco worker could earn a dollar an hour, compared with a dollar a day in the East, a restaurant meal cost three dollars. Even a bucket of water cost a dollar. A prospector paid ten dollars for a pick and five dollars for a tin pan. Ordinary boots cost $40 and having shirts washed cost $15 a dozen. Payment was required in advance. If the buyer had no cash, the seller would gladly take gold dust. In fact, coins were so scarce that a miner was sometimes forced to trade an ounce (31.1 grams) of gold (worth at least $16) for one silver dollar.

Of the 30,000 persons who arrived in 1849, 25,500 were men, 3,000 were women, and only 1,500 were children. A few families hoped to settle in the West and go into business or farm, but most intended to find a fortune and return home. Most of the men had boarded riverboats for Stockton and New Helvetia, then walked or rode "mud wagons" to the gold fields.

These **hordes** of argonauts turned John Sutter's life upside down. The first year's prospectors trampled his crops and killed his cattle for food. Defending his land claim in court—going all the way to the United States Supreme Court—took most of his money. **Creditors** eventually took his farm. Sutter died in Washington, D.C., in 1880, a poor and ruined man.

Mining towns were composed of people from around the world.

29

Hangtown, later Placerville, in the 1850s

As thousands of prospectors descended on the Sacramento, American, and Feather rivers, **ramshackle** mining camps arose overnight. They had names such as Poker Flat, Hangtown, Whiskey Bar, Hell's Delight, Git-up-and-Git, Skunk Gulch, and Dry Diggings. Many miners ended up with nothing, especially those who loved to gamble. But the rewards could be great. The first five prospectors on the Yuba River made $75,000 in three months. One lump of gold taken at Sonora weighed 28 pounds (12.7 kg). Eight nuggets from the same area weighed more than 20 pounds (9 kg) apiece. Even the workers who stayed at the Coloma sawmill found $25 to $30 in gold every day for several months.

At first prospectors picked small pieces of gold from shallow water. Flour-like gold "dust" could be found in rivers flowing into the Sacramento and San Joaquin valleys. This form of gold was easy to collect by **placer** mining. The miner shoveled dirt into a "washing pan," twirled it with water to wash off the gravel, and poured the water off. A few heavy specks of gold remained in the pan.

In deeper streams, the miner used a "**cradle**" or "rocker," a device about 2 to 3 feet (.6 to .9 m) long. One miner rocked it gently, while adding gravel with his hand. A second man brought more gravel. Flecks of gold became trapped against **riffles** at one end. A larger device, a "**sluice box**" or "**long tom**," was 12 feet (3.6 m) long by 8 inches (20.3 cm) deep. Miners shoveled dirt into the other end, and water carried lighter material away, trapping the gold. Using a cradle, two men could process 5 square yards (4.2 sq m) of gravel a day, while three men working a sluice box could handle 12 square yards (10 sq m) a day.

Men shoveling dirt into a sluice box

HOW THE GOLD GOT THERE

Near the Earth's center, rock is so hot that it is **molten**. Minerals, including gold, are present in this **magma**. The Sierra Nevada Mountains were once underwater. As they pushed upward, magma had **welled up** and then cooled and cracked. It formed a band of quartz in the foothills with ribbon-like **veins** or **lodes**, which contained gold-bearing **ore**. California miners discovered the network of veins of **quartz** in the Sierra Nevada Mountains and named it the "**Mother Lode.**" **Groundwater** and streams washed the ore for millions of years, releasing the gold. In summer, when streams have less water, bars of gravel containing gold dust and nuggets can be exposed.

Gold in its ribbon-like vein form

Geologists have estimated that miners in 1848-1849 took 502,940 ounces (14,258 kg) of gold from California. Most of it ended up in the Federal **mint**. It was used to make coins held as **bullion** reserves. In the 1860s, much of it went to pay the costs of the **Civil War**.

These methods of collecting gold were inexpensive, but by 1850, as the "easy pickings" began to run out, gold became harder to remove. The

Manual tools were soon replaced by large machines.

remaining gold was locked in **deposits** of **quartz** or buried beneath layers of soil and rock laid down over centuries. Crushing mills had to be built, and the quartz had to be crumbled so the gold could be separated out in a layer with the use of **mercury**. Mine shafts had to be sunk if the ore was 50 feet (15.2 m) down or deeper. In these cases, eastern **capitalists** provided the money while miners did the work.

Soon only companies with expensive machinery were mining. They had to dig deep into the earth, and use huge **dredges** to sift through riverbeds or tear up dry gravel beds. Their day over, many of the early prospectors headed for other states, where rumors of easy gold and silver were in the air.

Prospectors soon left when giant machines like dredges took over.

Using **hydraulic** mining, companies forced water and gravel from the bottom of streams through a nozzle like a garden hose but with much greater force. Bits of gold were then recovered from the loose gravel. This practice damaged rivers, harbors, and farmland by washing huge amounts of soil and gravel into the lowlands. Farmers had to fight the mining companies in court to save their lands.

(Above) a man using a nozzle to spray water. (Below) the pipe leading from the tank runs water to the sluice or nozzle.

Hydraulic mining causes major environmental problems.

In 1852, the peak year of the Gold Rush, the mining companies took more than $81 million worth of gold from the foothills. This amounted to nearly four million ounces (113,400 kg) of gold. A year later, $70 million worth of gold was removed. Between 1865 and 1885, gold production varied from $15 to $20 million a year. In 1900, it fell to $11 million.

MINTING COINS IN SAN FRANCISCO

The first known gold minted in San Francisco was a $5 gold piece produced at Benicia City on May 31, 1849. In the 1990s, one of these early coins was worth $1,200 to $10,000, depending on its condition. These were not official United States coins, but they worked just as well. In 1854, the United States Mint opened a branch in San Francisco.

Chapter IV: **A STATE FOUNDED ON GOLD**

The discovery of gold brought almost instant statehood to California. Most of the new western regions had been **territories** for years, administered by Congress. But the 30,000 people who had rushed to California in 1849 were determined to control their future. With people flooding in, Californians badly needed a system of law and order.

African-American slaves were brought to California, and by 1852, nearly 2,000 free African Americans lived there. They stayed in cities where **prejudice** was not as strong as in mining camps. President Zachary Taylor urged residents to draw up a constitution and apply for statehood. California's residents voted to become a state in late 1849. The question was, would California be a free state or a slave state? After passionate debate, Congress passed the **Compromise of 1850**, which let California enter the union as a free state. On September 9, 1850, Congress officially made California the 31st state.

RULE OF THE CAMPS

By 1860, most European Americans who had come to California lived near San Francisco or in mining camps. From the start, the camps had laws. Each prospector was to have an equal opportunity to dig and not be pushed aside. No individual could hold more than a single plot. The camp recorder kept a book showing the boundaries of each plot. But these **democratic** rules held only for white men. Jails did not exist. A person found guilty of a crime might be **banished** or **flogged**, have his ears cut off, or be hanged. In January 1849, so many hangings occurred in the camp named Dry Diggings that its name was changed to Hangtown. This town is now Placerville.

The laws of the camps were ignored when those in charge found them inconvenient.

When California had belonged to Mexico, European-American settlers had respected the Californios. But after the discovery of gold, the dark-skinned, Spanish-speaking people became one of the many groups that suffered **discrimination**. Shortly after California became a state, the legislature passed a Foreign Miners Tax of $20 a month for the right to mine. It was applied mainly to Mexicans, even though by treaty they were **naturalized** citizens. European Americans took over Californios' ranchos, subdividing them into farms. **Lynchings**, beatings, and robbery of Mexican and Mexican-American miners occurred frequently. By 1850, most Californios had abandoned the gold fields, and many headed south to Mexico.

Before 1848, there were almost no Chinese in California. But the news reached China before the end of the year, and before 1852, 25,000 Chinese had arrived. Most of them spoke little English. Because their religion was not Christianity, they were considered different and open to **suspicion**. European Americans chased Chinese miners from the gold fields, accusing them of stealing jobs and driving down wages. In 1854, they put forth a proposal to keep the Chinese out, and less than 30 years later Congress passed a law halting Chinese **immigration**.

The saddest fate belonged to the few hundred Native Americans who still lived in the Sierra Nevada mountains. Some had helped mine the gold with willow baskets in the early days, occasionally for themselves but usually for landowners with claims. With the huge swarm of prospectors in 1849, Native Americans were either killed or forced aside. Some groups, such as the **Yokut** tribe on the Fresno River, reluctantly signed treaties and settled on reservations. But others fiercely resisted losing their homelands. The last to surrender were the **Yosemite**, a Native group that had lived for centuries in the valley now known as Yosemite National Park.

After California became a state, many groups such as Chinese miners became targets for discrimination.

After state forces captured Yosemite Chief **Teneiya** and killed his son in 1851, he finally brought his people out of the mountains and signed a treaty.

The demand for supplies in the gold fields boosted industries in other states. Farms in Oregon's Willamette Valley sent fresh vegetables to San Francisco. Kit Carson and other retired mountain men drove sheep (6,500 sheep in 1853) from New Mexico to California to supply the market for wool. Texas cowboys and Mormons from Utah drove herds of cattle to the West Coast.

At the end of 1859, with civil war pending, the Federal government wanted to keep California in the **Union** and in close contact with Washington, D.C. **William Russell** proposed using swift horses in short **relays** to carry the mail. Thus, the **Pony Express** was born, promising mail delivery over the 1,966 miles (3,163 km) from St. Joseph, Missouri, to Sacramento in only 10 days. On April 3, 1860, riders left from both ends. In spite of blizzards, buffalo stampedes, and Indian attacks, each rider reached his destination on April 13.

Yosemite Valley, California, once home to the Yosemite tribe

By February 1861, war was certain, and key Californians seemed to sympathize with the **Confederates**. Strengthening the state's **alliance** with the Union depended on Lincoln's **Inaugural** Address reaching Sacramento as soon as possible. Russell's company spent $75,000 to prepare the Pony Express for this effort, hiring hundreds of men to set up posts along the route. The speech was **telegraphed** from Washington to Missouri and took only 7 days and 17 hours to get to Sacramento by Pony Express. California sided with the Union in the Civil War.

JAMES MARSHALL DIES

James Marshall died **penniless** in 1885 without making another important gold strike. Five years before he died, the state had refused him financial aid, but after he died the state spent $5,000 on a monument to him at Coloma.

But by October 1861, only 18 months after its historic beginning, the Pony Express was **obsolete**. Telegraph lines had been installed across the West. In 1869, the transcontinental railroad had been completed, joining east to west, while the Southern Pacific Railroad connected northern and southern states.

Although neither John Sutter nor James Marshall benefited in the end from the Gold Rush, another of the early pioneers did. **John Bidwell** had the **foresight** to realize that

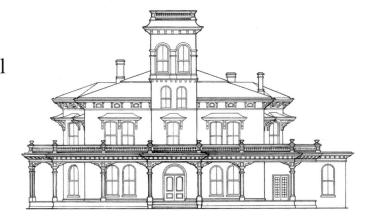

Bidwell mansion, Rancho Chico, California

California's true treasure was her productive land. Leading the first major wagon train caravan to California in 1841, he had found some gold on the Feather River. He used the money to buy 20,000 acres (8,100 hectares), and planted it in wheat, barley, and oats. He raised cattle, sheep, and horses and had an orchard with every kind of fruit and nut that would grow. Bidwell founded the town of Chico in 1860 and his home is now part of the California State Park system.

Bidwell, John (1819-1900) - American rancher and political figure who led the first wagon train to California in 1841.

Brannan, Samuel (1819-1889) - American printer who led a party of Mormon settlers to Yerba Buena (San Francisco) in 1846.

Carson, Kit (1809-1868) - American trapper, guide, and soldier; eventually superintendent of Indian affairs for Colorado Territory.

Foster, Stephen (1826-1864) - American composer who based some of his popular songs on African-American spirituals.

Marshall, James W. (1810-1885) - New Jersey carpenter who discovered gold at Sutter's sawmill on January 24, 1848, and started the California Gold Rush.

Mason, Richard B. (1797-1850) - American military governor of California (1847-1849).

Polk, James K. (1795-1849) - The 11th President of the United States (1845-1849).

Russell, William (1812-1872) - Head of Russell, Majors and Waddell, the company that founded the Pony Express.

Sutter, John (1803-1880) - Born Johann Sutter in Switzerland, emigrated to United States in 1834; he built a fort near Sacramento, California, in 1843.

Vallejo, Mariano (1808-1890) - Born in Monterey, California; he became military commander of Mexican California in 1838.

A TIMELINE OF THE HISTORY OF
— *The California Gold Rush* —

1821	Mexico wins independence from Spain.
1824-1847	The rancho period, during which Californios live a life of plenty.
1839	John Sutter arrives in California and develops a ranch, New Helvetia.
1841	First wagon train sets out on the Oregon Trail, with John Bidwell leading the California-bound settlers.
1848	The end of the Mexican War, in which the United States gains California.
1/24/1848	James Marshall finds gold at Sutter's sawmill.

3/15/1848	First notice of gold discovery appears in *The Californian.*
5/12/1848	Sam Brannan announces the discovery in the San Francisco streets, setting off "gold fever."
8/2/1848	Kit Carson arrives in Washington, D.C., with the news.
12/5/1848	President Polk, finally convinced, announces the gold find to Congress and the nation.
1849	Seeking gold in California, 30,000 argonauts travel the overland trails to California or arrive in San Francisco by ship. San Francisco's population zooms to 25,000.
10/13/1849	State Constitution approved in Monterey. State motto is to be "**Eureka.**"
11/10/1849	Since April 1, 1849, 697 ships have arrived in San Francisco. Of those, 401 are American and 296 are foreign.
12/31/1849	The population of San Francisco reaches 100,000.
1850	The Compromise of 1850 makes California the 31st state and postpones the Civil War.
1852	Peak year of production, with more than $81 million in gold taken from the Sierra Nevada foothills.
1854	First Federal mint branch opens in San Francisco.
1860-1861	The Pony Express is created and speeds mail between Missouri and San Francisco.
1861-1865	U.S. Civil War.
1869	Construction of a transcontinental railroad is completed.
1880	John Sutter dies in poverty.
1885	James Marshall dies in poverty, and the State of California erects a $5,000 monument to him at Coloma.

GLOSSARY

adobe - A building material made of dried earth or clay and straw.

alliance - Bond or connection; friendship.

argonaut - An adventurer engaged in a quest, especially one for gold.

avoirdupois - French for "goods of weight"; the units of weight based on a pound of 16 ounces (454 grams).

banish - To require to leave a country or place.

bankruptcy - The state of having lost all financial assets.

bullion - Gold or silver in bars, rather than coins.

Californio - One of the original Spanish colonists of California or their descendants.

Cape Horn - Southern tip of South America; said to resemble a horn in its shape.

capitalist - A person who invests money in business; a believer in the economic system that features private ownership of wealth.

cholera - A disease of humans and domestic animals caused by a poison produced by a comma-shaped bacterium.

Civil War - War between factions inside a country; the American Civil War (1861-1865) was fought partly over the right to own slaves.

Coloma - Native American group of the Sacramento Valley; town by that name.

composition - Makeup or arrangement.

Compromise of 1850 - A set of resolutions put forth by Senator Henry Clay of Kentucky in 1850 to prevent civil war.

Confederate - An alliance; the group of southern states that seceded from the United States and fought the Union Army in the Civil War.

coronet - A small crown or something that looks like a crown.

cradle - In mining, a device for sifting gold out of gravel.

creditor - A person to whom money or goods are owed.

decade - A period of 10 years.

democratic - Relating to or favoring democracy.

density - The mass (bulk) of a substance in a given volume or space.

deposit - In geology, matter laid down by a natural process.

discrimination - Differing treatment of individuals or groups on some basis other than merit.

dismal - Causing gloom or depression.

dredge - A machine or barge for removing earth using buckets on a chain or a suction tube.

ductile - Capable of being drawn out or hammered thin without breaking.

encyclopedia - A work that contains information on all branches of knowledge.

epidemic - Something which affects a large number of individuals, spreading among them rapidly.

eureka - An exclamation of excitement upon discovery; supposedly said by the Greek mathematician Archimedes (287-212 BC), when he discovered how to test the purity of gold.

exaggerate - To overstate or enlarge beyond the truth.

flog - To beat with a rod or whip.

foresight - The act or power of seeing or understanding in advance.

forty-niner - A person taking part in the 1849 California Gold Rush.

geologist - One who studies the history of the Earth, especially as recorded in rocks.

grain - A unit of weight based on the weight of a grain of wheat; one grain equals 0.0648 gram in the metric system.

groundwater - Water within the Earth that supplies wells and springs.

headrace - A channel that carries water into an industrial facility such as a mill.

Hispanic - Relating to Spanish or Spanish-American people living in the United States.

horde - A swarm or crowd.

hydraulic - Relating to water or other moving liquid.

immigrant - A person who moves into a country from somewhere else.

immigration - Movement into one country or place from another.

inaugural - Marking a beginning; relating to ceremonies that initiate someone into office.

lease - A rental contract; a piece of land or property that is leased.

lode - A rich ore deposit.

long tom - Nickname for a long sluice box used in placer mining.

lynch - To put to death (as by hanging) by mob action rather than by law.

magma - Melted rock material within the Earth.

mercury - A heavy silver-white metallic element that is liquid at ordinary temperatures.

Mexican War - Conflict between Mexico and the United States in 1846-1848.

mint - To make coins out of metal; a place where coins are made.

molten - Made by melting; made liquid by heat.

Mother Lode - The principal source or supply.

mountain man - An American frontiersman who usually began as a beaver trapper and ended up as an explorer, guide, or settler.

mythology - The myths (stories) dealing with the gods and legendary heroes of a people.

naturalize - To give the rights of a natural citizen, such as citizenship.

New Helvetia - John Sutter's ranch, named after the early people (*Helvetii*) of western Switzerland.

nugget - A solid lump of precious metal.

obsolete - Out-of-date, no longer useful.

Old Spanish Trail - Trail founded about 1776 to supply Spanish missions in California from Santa Fe, New Mexico.

ore - A mineral containing a valuable substance such as metal, which is mined.

Oregon Trail - Emigrant route to the Northwest from Independence, Missouri.

patron - The owner or master; the head of a household.

penniless - Without a penny; very poor.

pioneer - First in anything; one of the first to settle a territory.

placer - A natural deposit containing particles of valuable mineral, such as gold.

Pony Express - A relay mail service using fast saddle horses between St. Joseph, Missouri, and Sacramento, California, 1860-1861.

prejudice - Injury resulting from a decision or action that neglects one's rights.

prospector - Person who inspects a region for mineral deposits.

province - A part or region of a country managed by a central government.

quartz - Silicon dioxide in crystal form.

ramshackle - Poorly built, appearing about to collapse.

rancho - Spanish word for ranch.

relay - Relates to racing or working in teams with each team or rider covering a given portion of the course.

riffle - A cleat or bar fastened to a sloping surface in a gold-washing apparatus to catch and hold mineral grains.

Sierra Nevada - Spanish for "snowy saw-toothed mountains"; a high mountain system in eastern California.

sluice - An artificial passage for water with a valve or gate to regulate flow.

sluice box - A long, box-like structure used in placer mining.

Sonora Trail - Trail from the Gila River in Sonora, Mexico, to southern California, created by the Spanish in the 1770s to serve the California missions.

specific gravity - The ratio of the density of a substance to the density of water.

submerge - To put under water.

suspicion - The act of suspecting something wrong on slight evidence or none.

tailrace - A channel that carries used water away from an industrial facility such as a mill.

tall tale - Greatly exaggerated story; falsehood.

telegraph - A device for communicating at a distance, using coded signals.

Teneiya - Chief of the Yosemite group of Native Americans in the 1850s.

terrain - The physical features of the land in a region.

territory - A geographical area; in the United States, an area under its control, with a separate legislature but not yet a state.

Tomesha - "Ground afire" in Shoshonean; Native name for Death Valley, California.

transcontinental - Extending across a continent, such as a railway.

troy ounce - A unit of weight equal to 480 grains (31.1 grams); 12 troy ounces equal a pound (.373 kg).

Union - The group of states that opposed slavery in the American Civil War.

vein - In geology, a bed of mineral matter.

well up - To rise, as water in a well.

Yerba Buena - Spanish for "good herb" or peppermint; the original name of San Francisco, California.

Yokut - A tribe of Native Americans once numbering about 18,000 along the Fresno River.

Yosemite - A group of Southern Sierra Miwok Natives whose original home was the valley now known as Yosemite National Park.

INDEX

Books of Interest

Balmes, Kathy. *Thunder on the Sierra*, Silver Moon Press, 2001.

Ferris, Julie. *California Gold Rush: A Guide to California in the 1850s*, Larousse Kingfisher Chambers, 1999.

Gregory, Kristiana. *Seeds of Hope: Gold Rush Diary of Susanna Fairchild, California Territory, 1849*, Scholastic, 2003.

Hart, Eugene. *A Guide to the California Gold Rush*, Free Wheel Publications, 2002.

Roop, Connie and Peter, eds. *The Diary of David R. Leeper*, Benchmark Books, 2000.

Stanley, Jerry. *Hurry Freedom*, Crown Books for Young Readers, 2000.

Web Sites

http://www.kidport.com/RefLib/UsaHistory/CalGoldRush/CalGoldRush.htm

http://ceres.ca.gov/ceres/calweb/geology/goldrush.html

http://www.calgoldrush.com/index.html

http://www.ncgold.com/History/california-gold-rush.html

http://www.isu.edu/%7Etrinmich/home.html

Linda Thompson is a Montana native and a graduate of the University of Washington. She was a teacher, writer, and editor in the San Francisco Bay Area for 30 years and now lives in Taos, New Mexico. She can be contacted through her Web site,

http://www.highmesaproductions.com

48